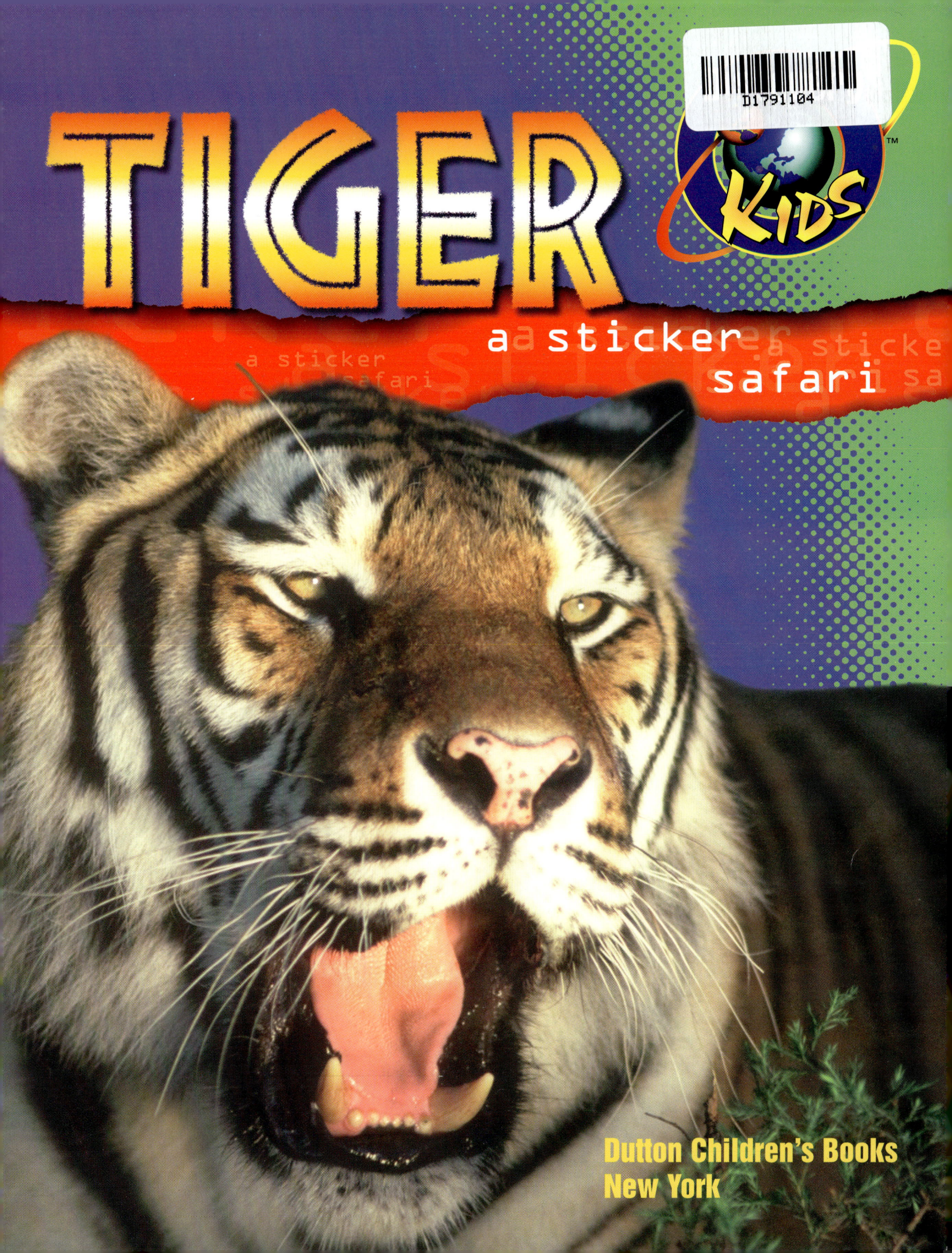

TIGER

a sticker safari

Dutton Children's Books
New York

All About Cats

You might not think the pet cat napping in the sun at your house has much in common with a 600-pound tiger. But it does. All cats are similar. They have agile bodies, good eyesight and hearing, sharp teeth and claws. Cats behave in similar ways, too, whether they're stalking a chew toy in your bedroom or an elk in a Siberian forest. Your cat belongs to a group known as the small cats, which includes the lynx, bobcat, cougar, and puma. The big cats are the lion, leopard, snow leopard, jaguar, and —

the tiger.

Leopard

Leopards have powerful front legs and are good climbers. They stay cool during the heat of midday by resting among the high, shady branches of trees. They also ambush prey from there, dropping down on pigs, antelope, monkeys, and other animals. After the kill, the leopard drags its victim high up into the tree, out of the reach of other hungry creatures. Leopards live in Africa, the Middle East, and Asia.

Snow leopard

The snow leopard lives in the snowy mountains of central Asia. Its thick, woolly fur keeps it warm. This cat is a great leaper, gracefully getting around the rocky ledges where it lives. A long tail helps the snow leopard balance as it jumps.

Lion

The lion is the only big cat that lives in a group. These groups, called prides, can have as many as twelve females and their cubs. The females do the hunting, but the males eat first. Male lions look different from females because of their bushy manes. No other big cats have manes. Perhaps this is why the male lion is known as the king of the jungle. Or maybe it's his roar—which is the loudest sound a cat can make. Lions live in Africa.

Cheetah

The cheetah is in a category of its own: It is neither a big cat nor a small one. It is the fastest land animal, able to run over 70 miles an hour—as fast as a car speeding on a highway. Big cats pounce on their prey, but the cheetah pulls its victim down after a fast chase. Cheetahs have retractable claws like other cats, but without the protective sheaths. Their exposed claws function like cleats, helping the cheetah grip. Cheetahs live in Africa and the Middle East.

Jaguar

The jaguar can weigh 250 pounds and is the largest cat in the Americas. It looks similar to the leopard, but it has a bigger head and body and shorter, thicker legs. The jaguar also has smaller spots, clustered in circles called rosettes. Jaguars live in Central and South America.

Tiger

The tiger is the biggest of the big cats, and it's in big trouble. Scientists estimate there may be as few as 5,000 wild tigers left in the world. Some species are already extinct. The rest of this book is about the species of tiger that still exist: the Siberian, Bengal, Sumatran, Indochinese, and Chinese.

The Biggest of

Ears
A tiger's large, rounded earflaps help direct sound waves down into the ear. And cats can rotate their ears to pick up sounds coming from different directions. They can even hear animals burrowing underground!

Eyes
Tigers have very good eyesight. In dim light, their pupils open wide to let in light. But the pupils will also expand if the tiger is frightened. Tigers can see color only during the day. At night, they see in black and white!

Tongue
Like all cats, the tiger has a rough, sandpaperlike tongue. The tiger uses its tongue like a comb to keep its fur clean. The spiky surface of the tongue is also good for licking meat off bones.

Teeth
A tiger's greatest weapon for killing prey is its long, curved teeth, called canines. A tiger's canine teeth can be 3 inches long! (Yours are about $1/4$ inch long.)

Jaws
Tigers have powerful jaws, but they can move them only from side to side, not up and down. That's why they chew on one side of their mouth, and tilt their head sideways as they eat.

Voice

Tigers, and all big cats, can purr, but they can't do it as well as small cats can. The cat at your house has a small bone at the base of its tongue that allows it to purr as it breathes in and out.

the Big

> The tiger is the biggest cat, and the Siberian is the biggest tiger.

Body
The body of the tiger is sturdy and graceful. An average tiger is 6 1/2 feet long and weighs 500 pounds. The biggest tiger is the Siberian, shown here. It can grow to 12 feet in length and weigh 700 pounds.

Claws
Tiger claws are made of keratin, the same material your fingernails are made of. All cats except cheetahs can pull back (retract) their claws. When a cat wants to use its claws, it flexes a muscle in its foot—and the claw comes out of its sheath.

Tail
A tiger's tail signals its feelings. Side to side means "I'm stalking." Up and down means "I'm mad." A tiger's tail can be half as long as its body.

Feet
Cats walk on their toes. The padding on the undersides of their feet allows them to move silently as they stalk prey. Perhaps you've tried this—walking on tiptoes when sneaking up on your little sister or brother?

That's why your cat purrs constantly when she's content. But big cats don't have this bone. They purr only when breathing out. But big cats can do something that small cats can't: ROARRR!!!

Growing Up Tiger

Tigers are giant cats, but they begin life very small. They weigh just two pounds when they are born, less than a human baby. A mother tiger usually gives birth to a litter of two to four cubs. These helpless little creatures will depend completely on their mother for food and protection until they are about two years old.

Bathtime
Keeping their fur and skin clean is important to cats. Any little wound could become a serious, troublesome infection. Before cubs learn to clean themselves, Mom gives them lots of licks to get rid of stray hairs and dirt. As she cleans, she spreads her unique scent to the cubs, marking them as part of her "territory."

Playtime
Cubs love to roughhouse, and their mother lets them. All that pouncing, nipping, and batting at one another is practice for the hunting they will do as grown tigers. And just like you, cubs play with "toys"—sticks, rocks, feathers. These objects are stand-ins for prey.

Earn your stripes
Tiger cubs have blurry markings at birth. It will be two years before they have the bold, distinctive stripes of mature tigers.

Food
Tiger cubs drink their mother's milk for the first six months of their lives and then eat meat that their mother brings them. But even before they are ready to chew, they will play happily with their mother's kill, pouncing and nipping at the dead animal. This is practice for when they will kill their own prey.

Latchkey cats

As a single parent, the female tiger will leave her cubs alone while hunting. She finds a den for them to hide in while she is away. Young tigers don't have the strength or speed to defend themselves from predators. Leopards, wild dogs, hyenas, and even snakes can snack on little cubs.

Tough to be a tiger

For all Mom's efforts, only about half of her cubs will survive to adulthood. Threats to cubs include starvation—if Mom can't find enough prey—and predators, including other tigers. Male tigers can be particularly aggressive. They will sometimes kill the cubs of another male so that they can mate with the female.

On their own

When cubs are two years old, they leave their mother to survive on their own. They must find their own hunting ranges. A daughter might choose land near her mother's, but a male tiger will search farther away, sometimes fighting with other males for prime land.

You can't go home again

If a young tiger ventures into her mother's territory, the mother will drive her away unless prey is plentiful. Then Mom might permit a visit. Grown female tigers sometimes share kills; male tigers, rarely.

Habitat and

Tigers live where there are plenty of trees, bushes, and tall grass. They need shade, and they need a place where they can blend in with the environment and not be seen easily by the prey they stalk.

Out in the cold
For the Siberian tiger, home is the snowy forests of Siberia in Russia.

Stripes
No two tigers have the same stripe pattern, but all tigers have stripes for the same reason. Stripes provide camouflage in tall grass and in dappled forests.

Taking a dip
Unlike other cats, tigers love water. In warm climates, they keep cool by lying in water. They sometimes even catch fish and crabs to eat! But tigers don't like getting their face wet. They usually back into the water to avoid it.

Territory

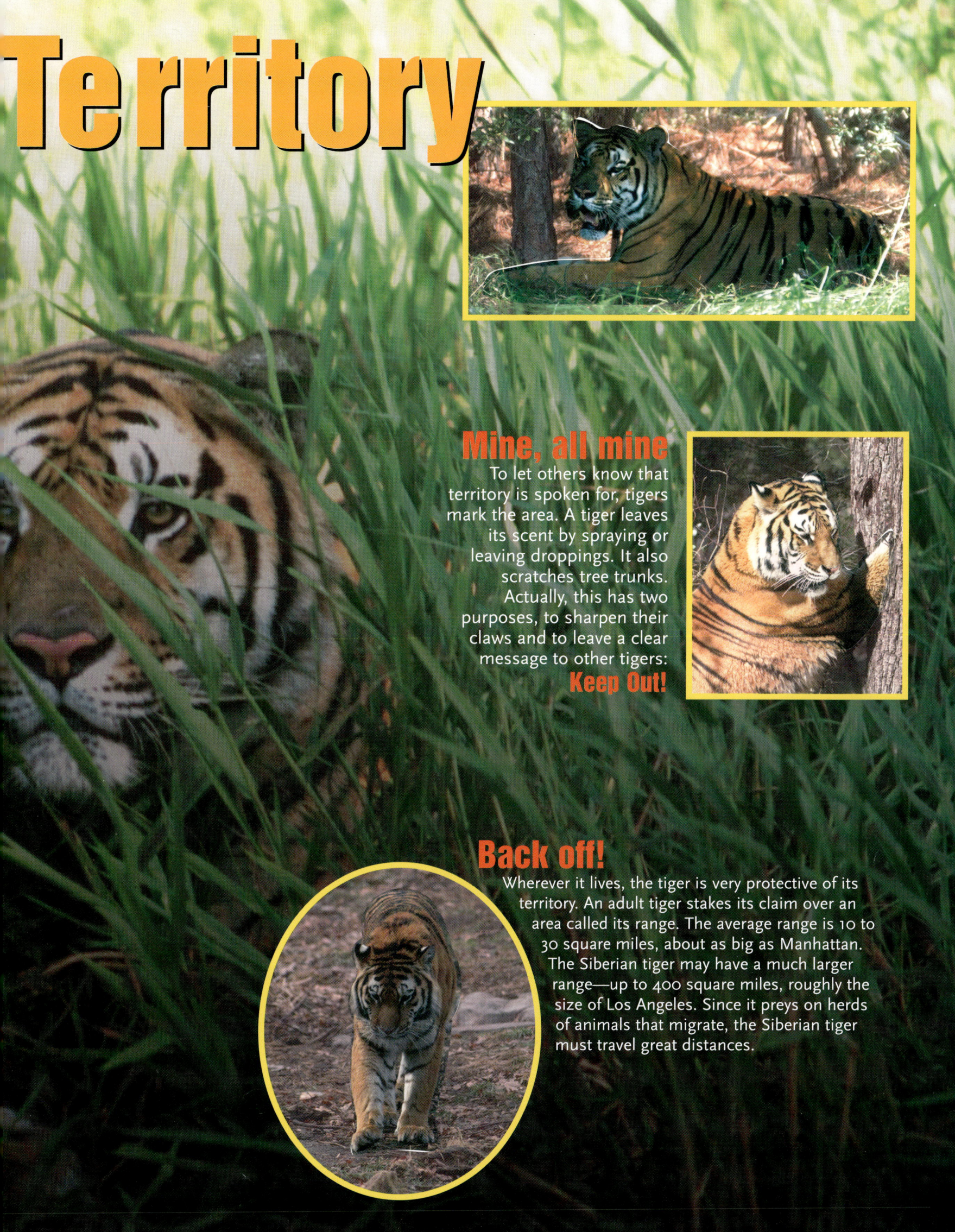

Mine, all mine
To let others know that territory is spoken for, tigers mark the area. A tiger leaves its scent by spraying or leaving droppings. It also scratches tree trunks. Actually, this has two purposes, to sharpen their claws and to leave a clear message to other tigers: **Keep Out!**

Back off!
Wherever it lives, the tiger is very protective of its territory. An adult tiger stakes its claim over an area called its range. The average range is 10 to 30 square miles, about as big as Manhattan. The Siberian tiger may have a much larger range—up to 400 square miles, roughly the size of Los Angeles. Since it preys on herds of animals that migrate, the Siberian tiger must travel great distances.

Tigers Then and

Cats have been around for about 5 million years. Perhaps their best-known cat ancestor is the saber-toothed tiger. This big-fanged early cat, which wasn't really a tiger, died out 10,000 years ago. But other big cats continue to be top predators on their continents, like the tiger in Asia. There are five subspecies of tiger, but their numbers are small and growing smaller. If action isn't taken to protect them, your children will only know tigers in zoos.

Saber-toothed tiger

There were many saber-toothed cats through the ages, but the most famous is Smilodon, one of the largest cats the world has ever known. It lived in North and South America. Its fangs were 6 inches long. (That's as long as your forearm!) It didn't bite its prey by bringing its jaws together but drove those giant teeth into its luckless victim with a powerful downward thrust of its head, neck, and shoulders. Humans might have been among its prey. The Smilodon disappeared just 10,000 years ago.

Sumatran tiger

This tiger, which lives only on the island of Sumatra in Indonesia, has the darkest coat of all tigers. It also has the most stripes, which are black and spaced close together. The Sumatran is the smallest tiger; it can grow to 8 feet long and weigh 265 pounds. It is believed there are about 500 Sumatran tigers left on the island, mostly in national parks.

Tiger tales

Tigers inspire awe. The Annamites, an ancient Southeast Asian people, thought that different-colored tigers ruled the four directions and seasons.

*The red tiger ruled the south and summer.

Now

Bengal tiger
Most Bengal tigers live in India and its surrounding countries. There are more Bengals in the wild than other types. Still, there are fewer than 5,000. Males can reach 9 1/2 feet in length and weigh 480 pounds.

Siberian tiger
The Siberian, also called the Amur, lives mostly in eastern Russia. It has pale orange fur, brown stripes with wide spaces in between, and thick white fur around its neck. The biggest tiger ever recorded was a Siberian male. It weighed 1,025 pounds—as much as a grand piano! In the 1940s, there were just 24 Siberian tigers in the wild. Now there are close to 500, but the Siberian is still endangered.

White tiger
This unusual creature is not a separate subspecies. White tigers, which have blue eyes and brown stripes, are actually Bengal tigers. White cubs are born to parents that both carry the gene for white coloring. Breeders have increased the population of white tigers, which are a popular attraction at zoos. Some people who are working to save tigers think this is a mistake, since the animals are being bred for entertainment rather than preservation.

Tigers in captivity
There are more tigers living in circuses, zoos, and private reserves than there are in the wild. Some captive tigers live in small, caged areas, but many live in well-designed habitats, where they are protected from poachers and can be studied by scientists. Maybe what scientists learn can be used to help save other tigers.

*The black tiger ruled the north and winter.

*The blue tiger ruled the east and spring.

*The white tiger ruled the west and autumn.

The Facts on

FREEZE! Have you seen movies with a scene like this one? A character is surprised by a deadly creature—snake, grizzly bear, dinosaur—and a nearby guide urges the frightened person to "Keep still!" Well, when it comes to the tiger, this is good advice. A tiger's hunting instincts are triggered by movement. So keeping still will keep the tiger still, too. But tigers are willing to wait for any signs of scurrying!

It's an ambush!

Tigers keep hidden under the cover of grass or bushes until they are close enough to their prey to pounce, usually about 20 feet away. Surprise is important, for though tigers can run up to 30 miles an hour, this is only in short bursts. A running deer can outlast them. However, a distracted deer might not have time to run.

Man-eaters

Tigers are considered the most dangerous of the big cats. In the early part of the 1900s, about 900 people a year in India were said to have been killed by tigers. These incidents are rare today. There are fewer tigers, but also people are being more cautious in tiger territory. Most tiger attacks occur when people wander into a tiger's range. As the big cats' forest homes are turned into farmland and villages, tigers and humans could come into more life-threatening contact.

Two-faced folks

Tigers usually attack from behind. In the Sundarbans mangrove forests of India, workers who enter to cut down trees wear masks of human faces on the back of their head. This may confuse any tiger creeping up from behind into thinking that the workers are actually facing in its direction.

Attacks

It's a drag.
Tigers prefer to eat in privacy, so they will drag their prey into the bushes before munching. A single adult tiger has the pulling power of thirty men; it can drag more than 1,000 pounds of meat for hundreds of yards!

Chow time
Tigers can eat 100 or more pounds of meat at a time, then they might not eat again for three or four days. Do your parents save leftovers? Well, so do tigers. They will stash the rest of a meal under bushes until they are hungry again. Hiding their meat keeps scavengers like vultures, wild dogs, and other tigers from finding it.

You better watch out!
Tigers do their hunting at night when other animals—their prey—cannot see very well. Like pet cats, tigers have excellent vision. Their eyes have a special part that reflects any available light into the inner eye, helping them to see about six times better than we can in the dark.

Favorite tiger prey

chital (spotted deer)
swamp deer
sambar deer
buffalo
cattle
wild boars
antelope

But also:
langur monkeys
frogs
fish
porcupines

Lands of the Tiger

In the last century there were more than 100,000 tigers left in the wild. Now there are just 5,000 to 7,000. Every day a tiger is killed, sometimes by poachers, sometimes by farmers protecting their livestock. But tigers also die because they are running out of places to live. Each tiger needs many miles of forest, full of prey. As the forests of Asia disappear, so will the tiger.

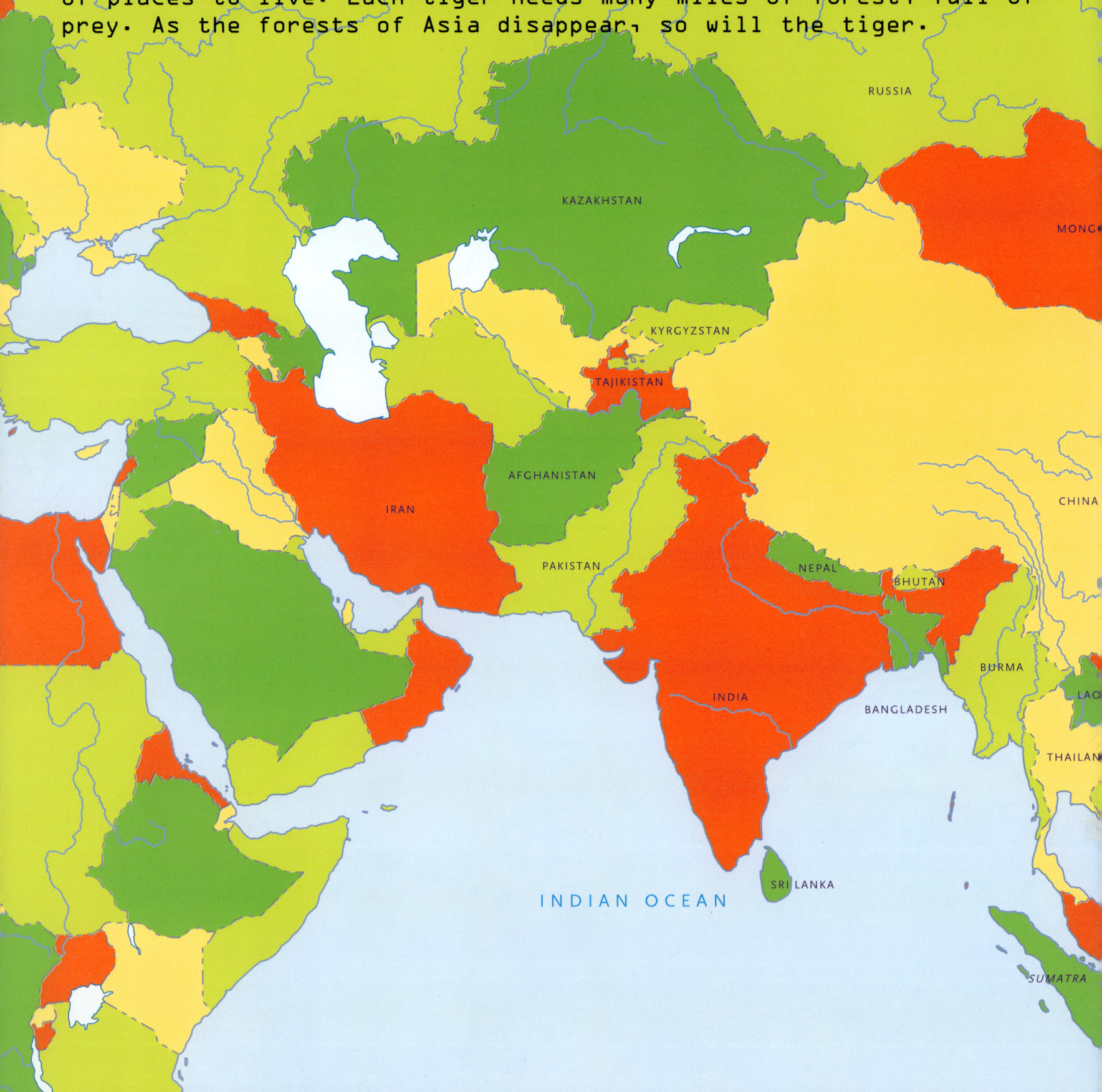

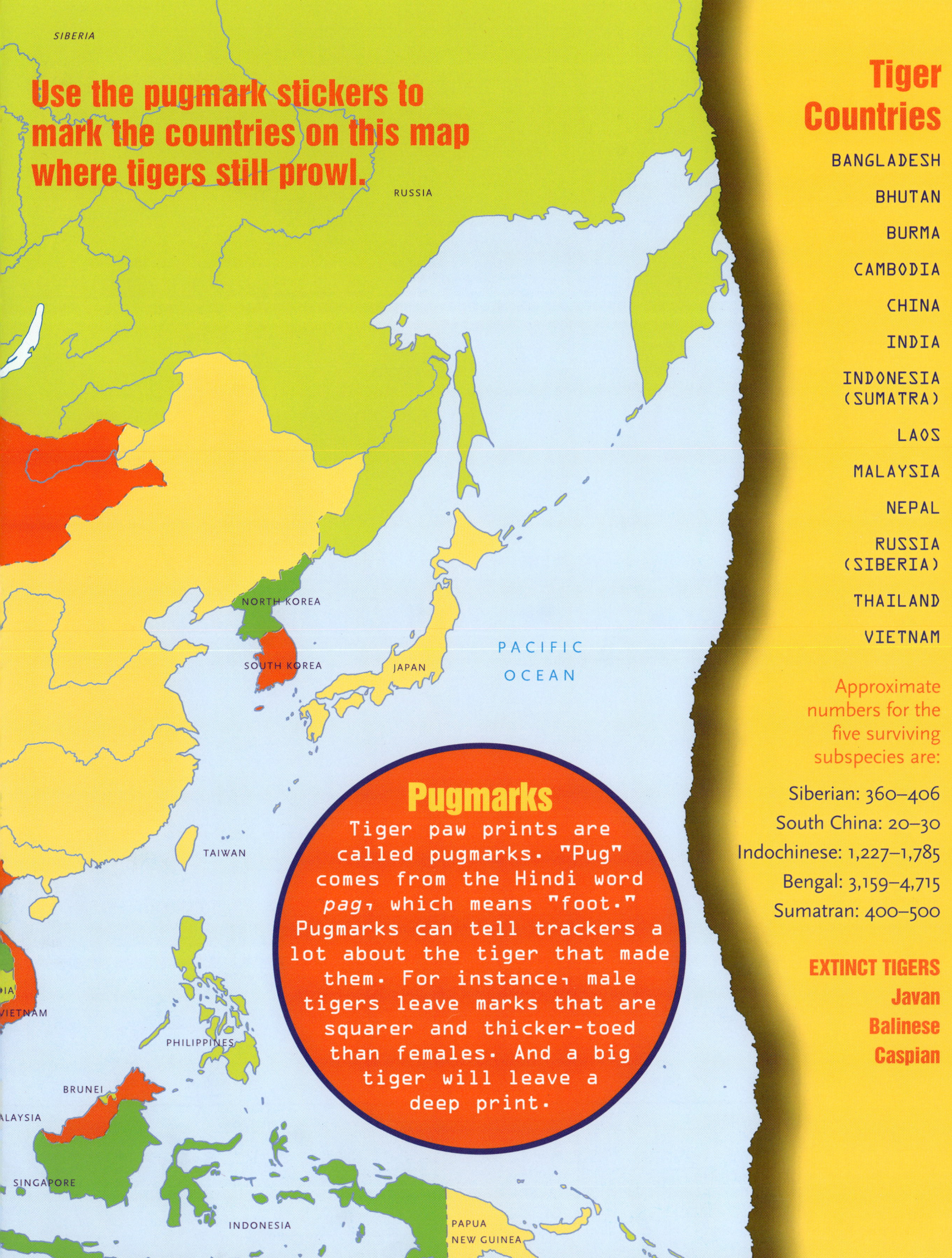

Find Out More

There are many organizations that support and fight to protect the tiger. Here are some addresses and Web sites you can use to find out more about tigers and the efforts to save them.

Discovery Kids Online
www.discoverykids.com
Discovery Kids™ has a kid-friendly Web site with lots of information about tigers and other animals.

The Tiger Information Center
www.5tigers.org

All for Tigers!
www.tiger.to

Tiger Eyes
www.tigereyes.com

Tiger Town
www.best.com/~hazelh.tiger.html

Save the Tiger Fund
National Fish and Wildlife Foundation
1120 Connecticut Ave, NW
Suite 900
Washington, DC 20036
(202) 857-0166
(202) 857-0162 fax
tiger@nfwf.org

Hornocker Wildlife Institute, Inc.
P.O. Box 3246
University of Idaho
Moscow, Idaho 83843-1908
1-888-Tiger44
208-885-6871
Fax: 208-885-2999
www.uidaho.edu/rsrch/hwi/main.html

The Tiger Foundation
Suite 1200, 543 Granville Street
Vancouver, British Columbia
Canada V6C 1X8
Phone: (604) 893-8718
Fax: (604) 685-2838
E-mail: info@tigers.ca
www.tigers.ca

Photo Credits:
Pages 4-5:
Photo 12: CORBIS/David A. Northcott
Photo 14: CORBIS/Terry Whittaker; Frank Lane Picture Age

Pages 6-7:
Background and Photo 18: CORBIS/Tom Brakefield
Photo 16: CORBIS/Terry Whittaker; Frank Lane Picture Age
Photos 17 and 22: CORBIS/D. Robert Franz

Photos 19 and 23: CORBIS/Terry Whittaker; Frank Lane Picture Age
Photo 20: CORBIS/Dow and Hedren
Photo 21: CORBIS/Bryn Colton; Assignments Photography

Pages 8-9:
Photo 26: CORBIS/Terry Whittaker; Frank Lane Picture Age
Photo 27: CORBIS/W. Perry Conway

Pages 10-11:
Photo 32: Transparency number: 1017(2) (Smilodon by Charles R. Knight) Courtesy Department of Library Services, American Museum of Natural History
Photo 33: CORBIS/Lynda Richardson
Photo 35: CORBIS/Richard Hamilton Smith
Photo 36: CORBIS/Tom Brakefield
Photo 37: CORBIS/Kelly-Mooney Photography

Pages 12-13:
Photo 43: CORBIS/Sheldon Collins